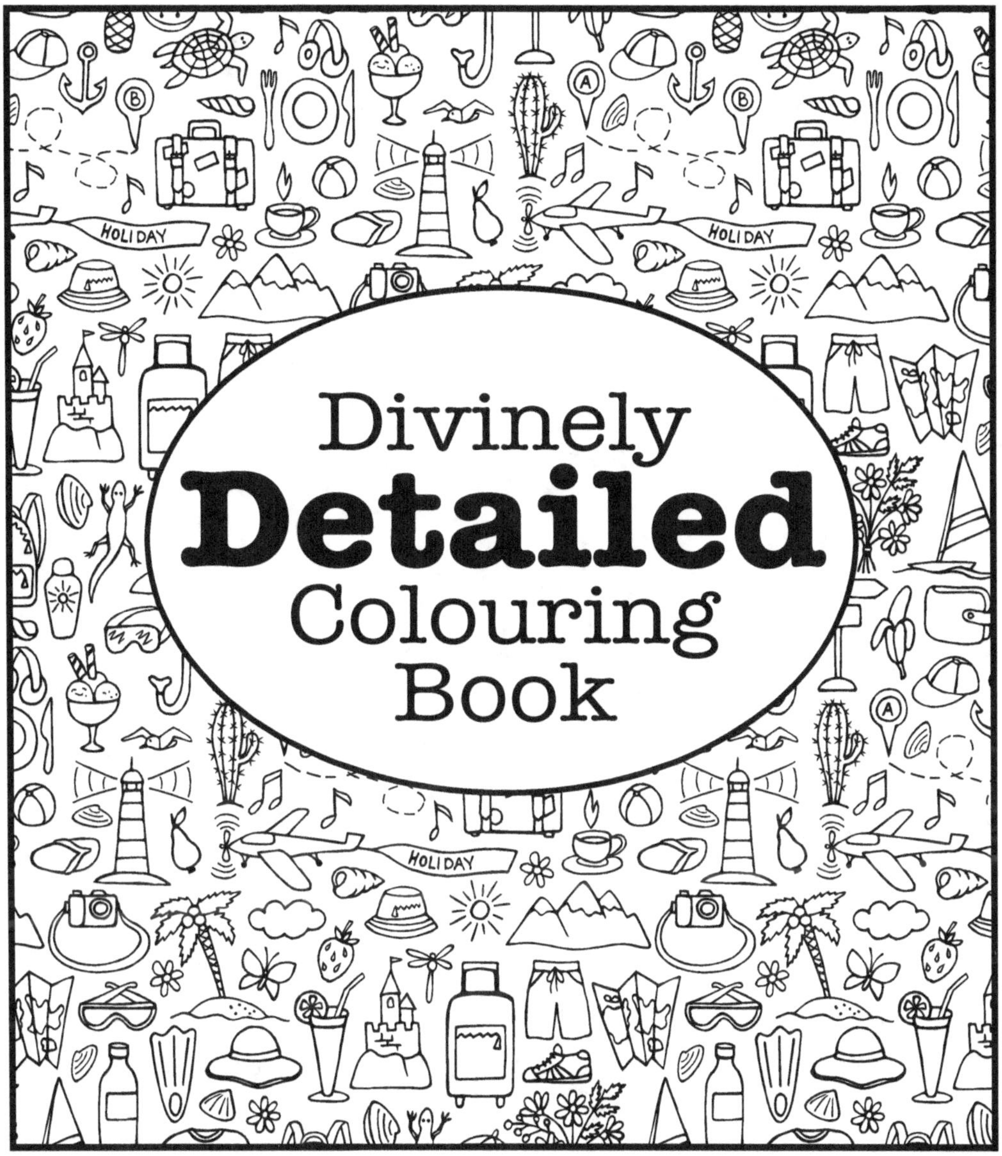

Divinely Detailed Colouring Book

Divinely Detailed Colouring Book 8

First published in 2016 by Kyle Craig Publishing

Copyright © 2016 Kyle Craig Publishing

Design: Elizabeth James, Julie Anson, Alison McNicol, Natalia Toropova, Shutterstock, Inc.

ISBN: 978-1-78595-111-4

A CIP record for this book is available from the British Library.

A Kyle Craig Publication

www.kyle-craig.com

All Rights Reserved.

No part of this publication may be reproduced, stored in a retrieval system or transmitted by any form or by any means, electronic, recording or otherwise without the prior permission in writing from the publishers.

Unauthorised reproduction of any part of this publication by any means including photocopying is an infringement of copyright.

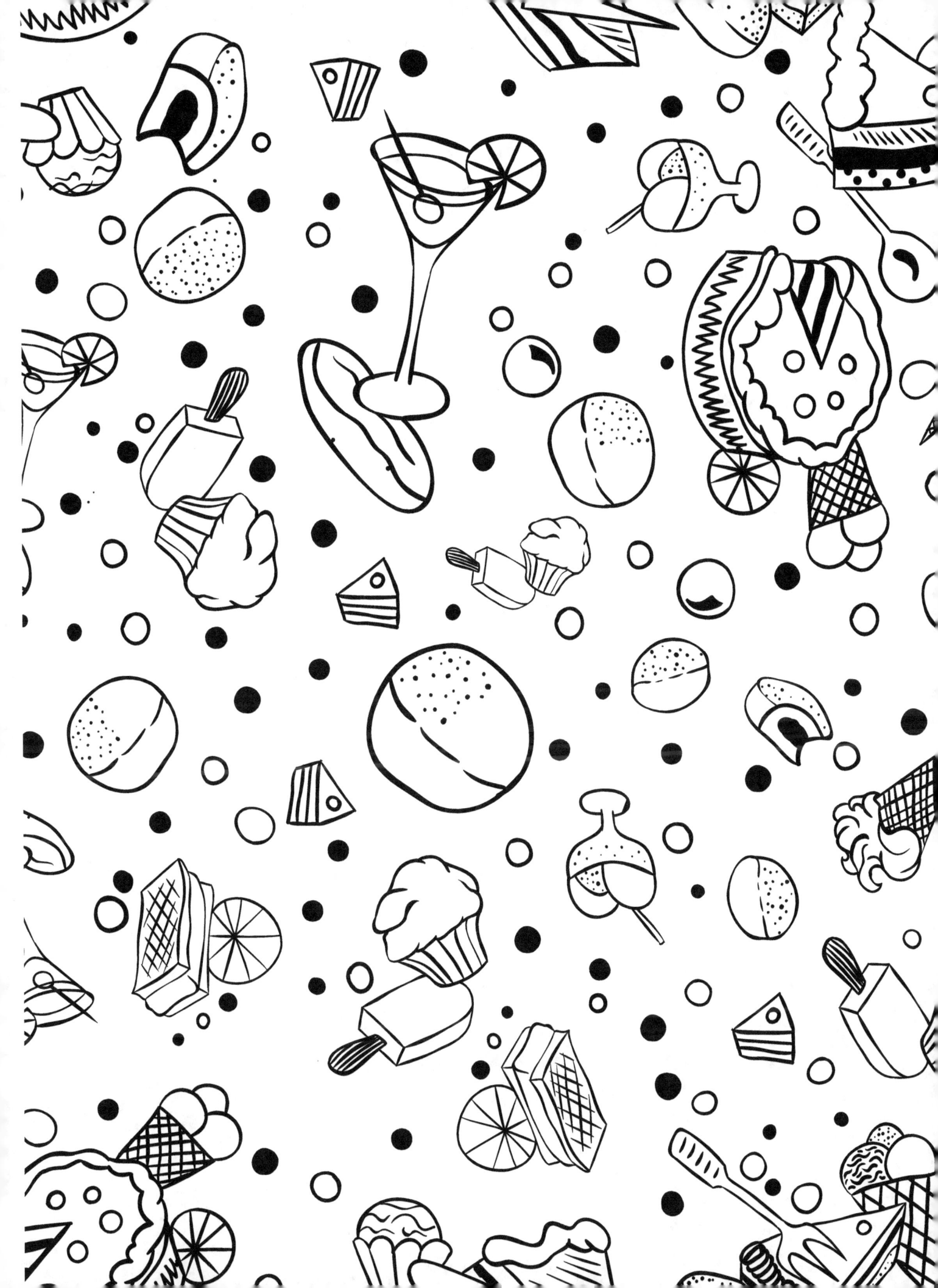

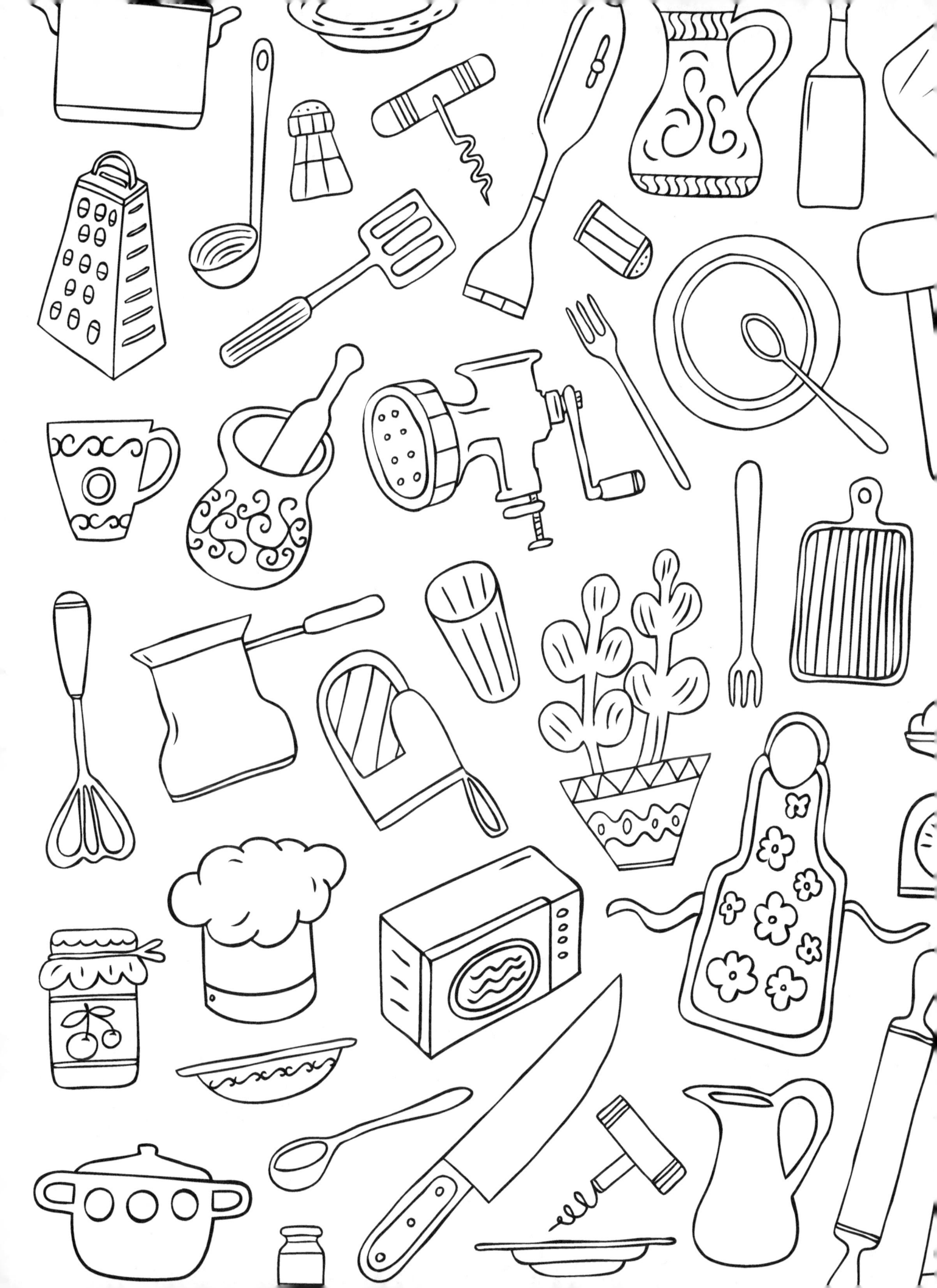

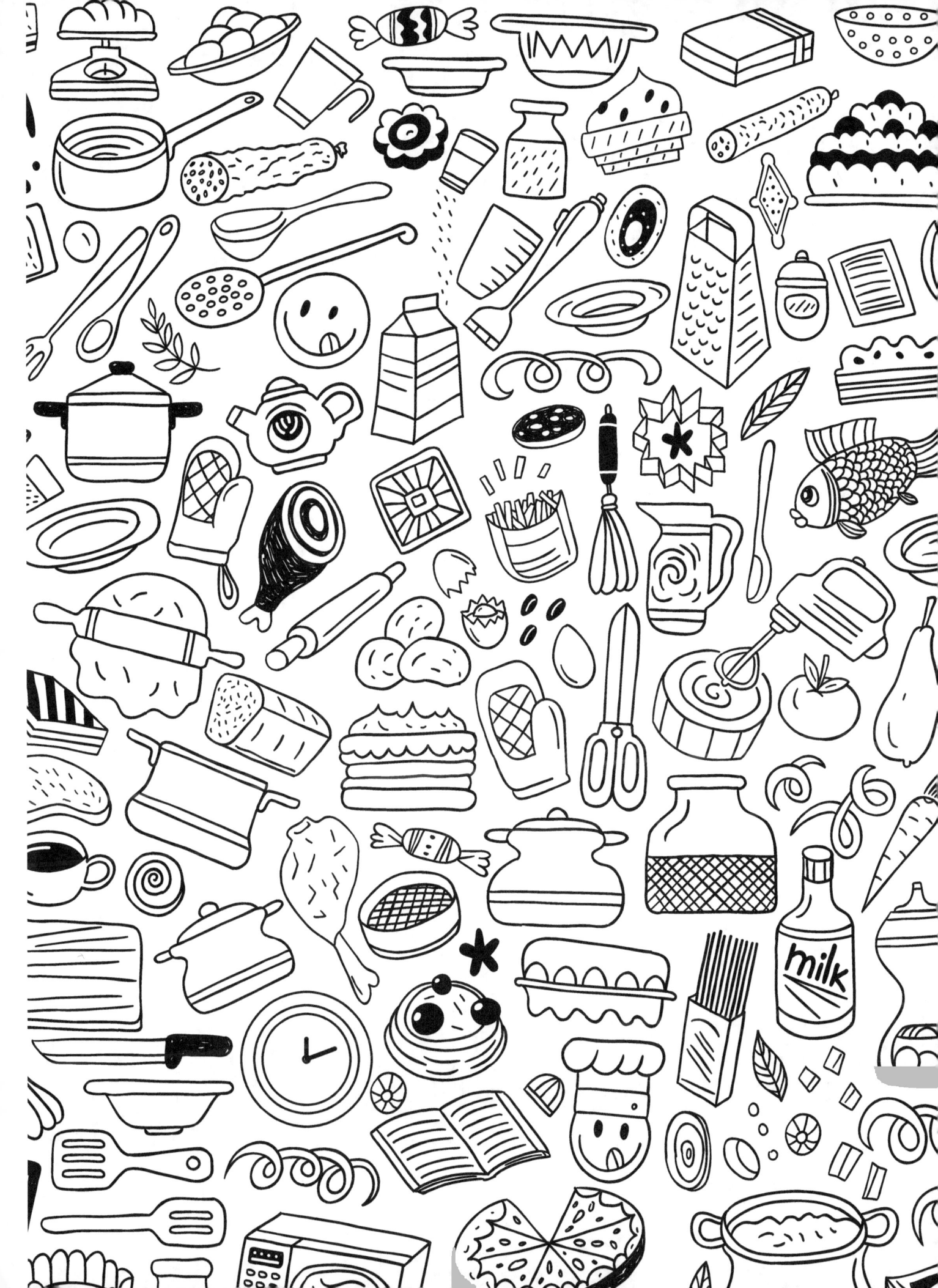

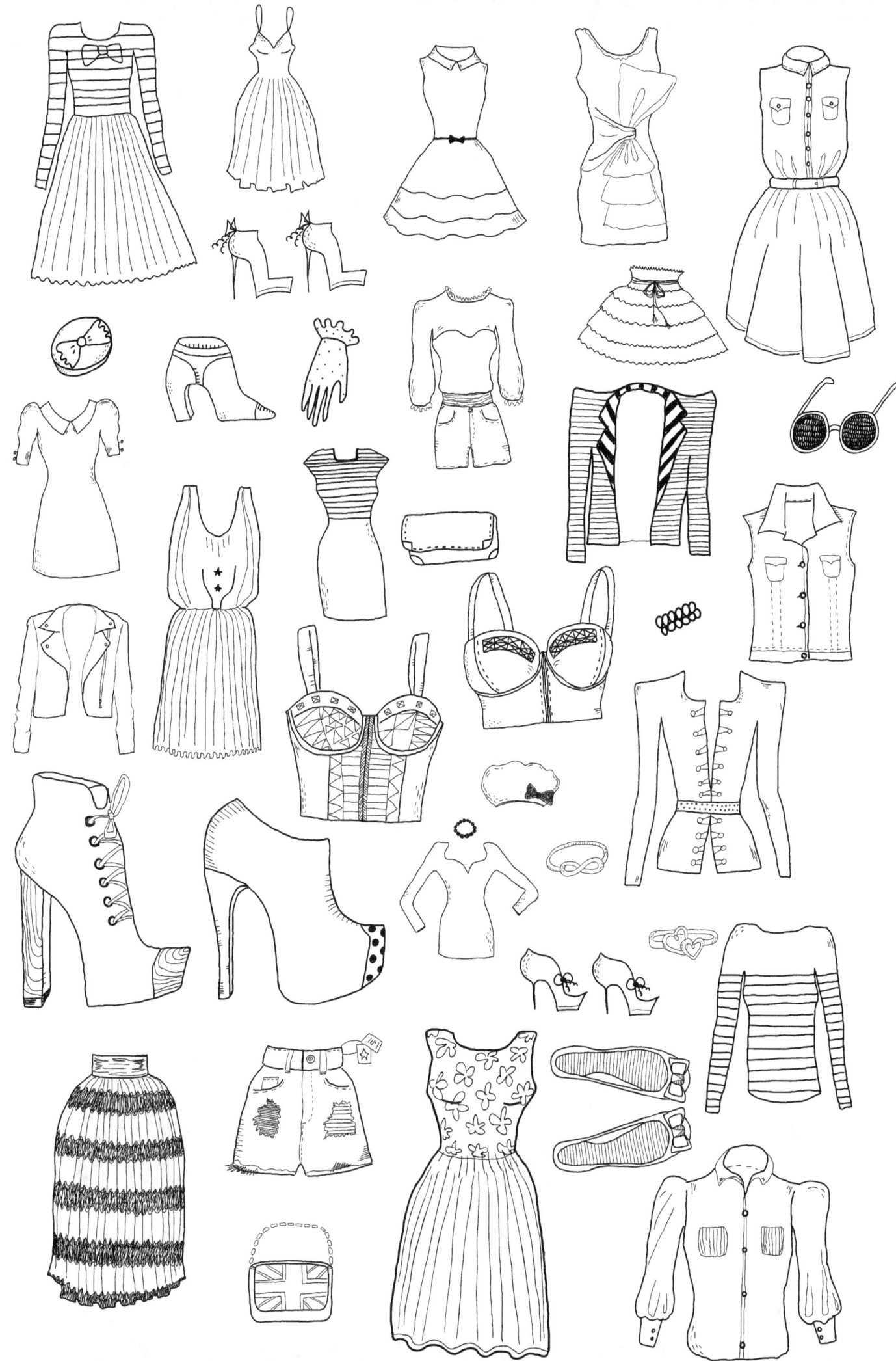

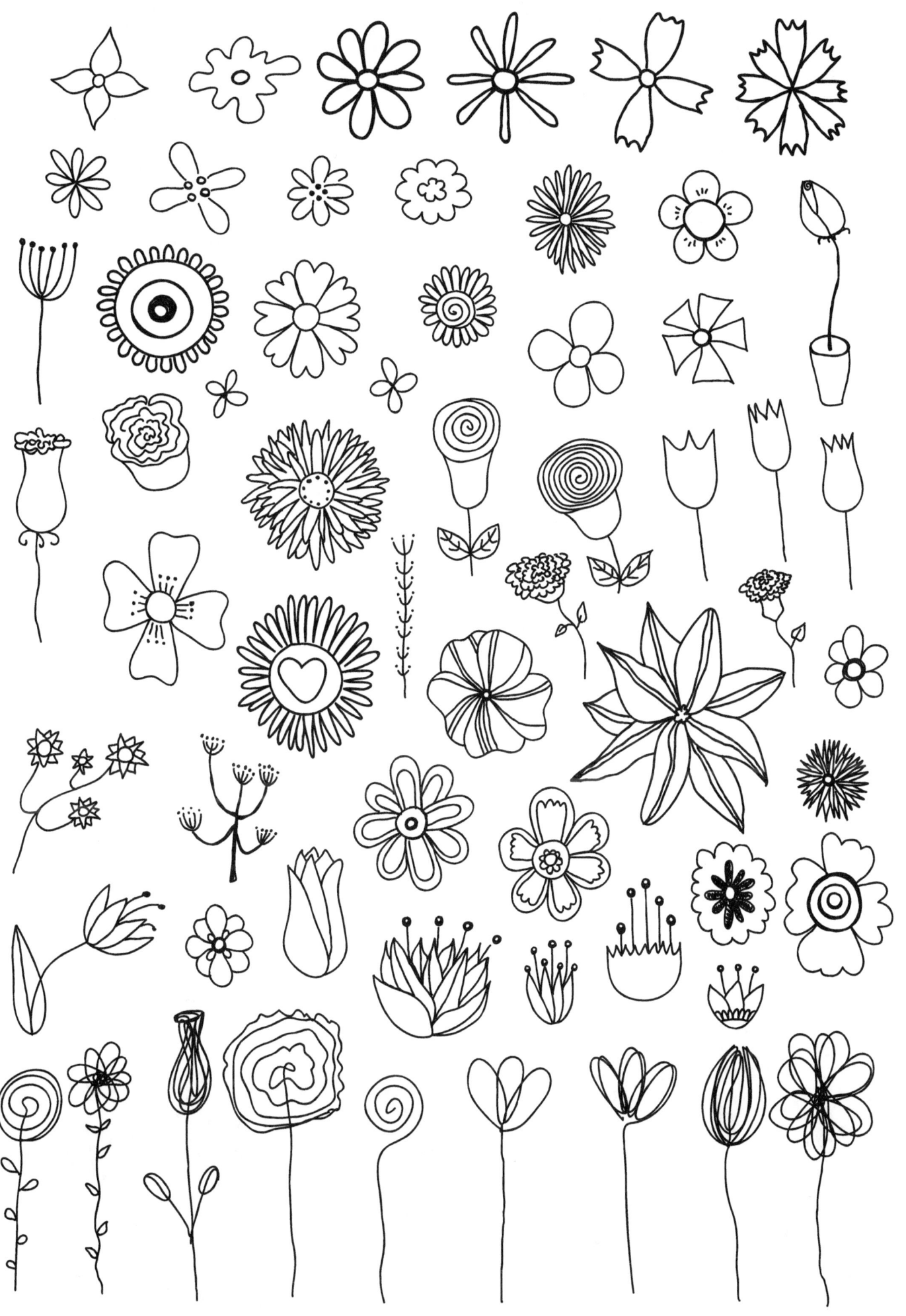

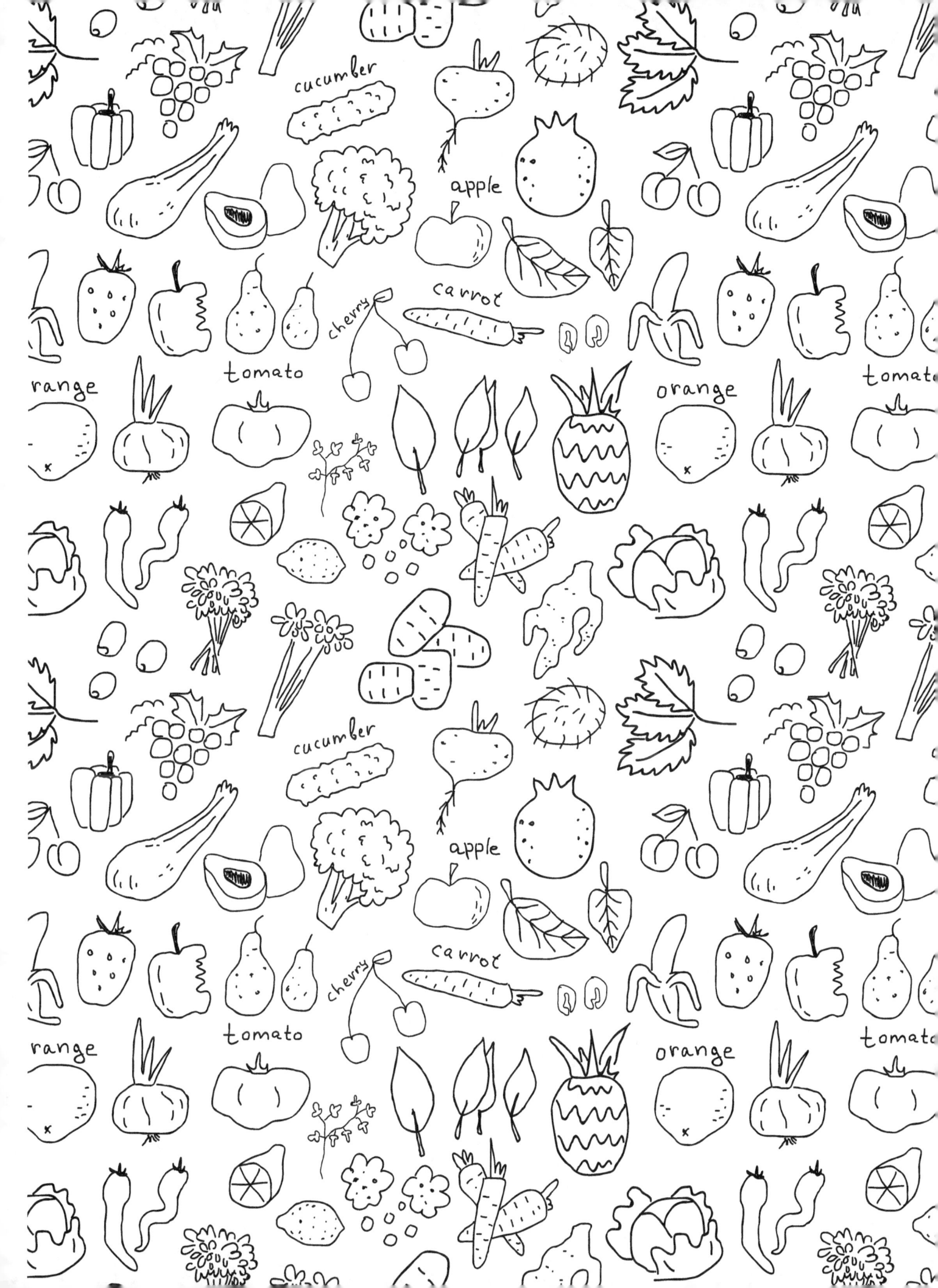

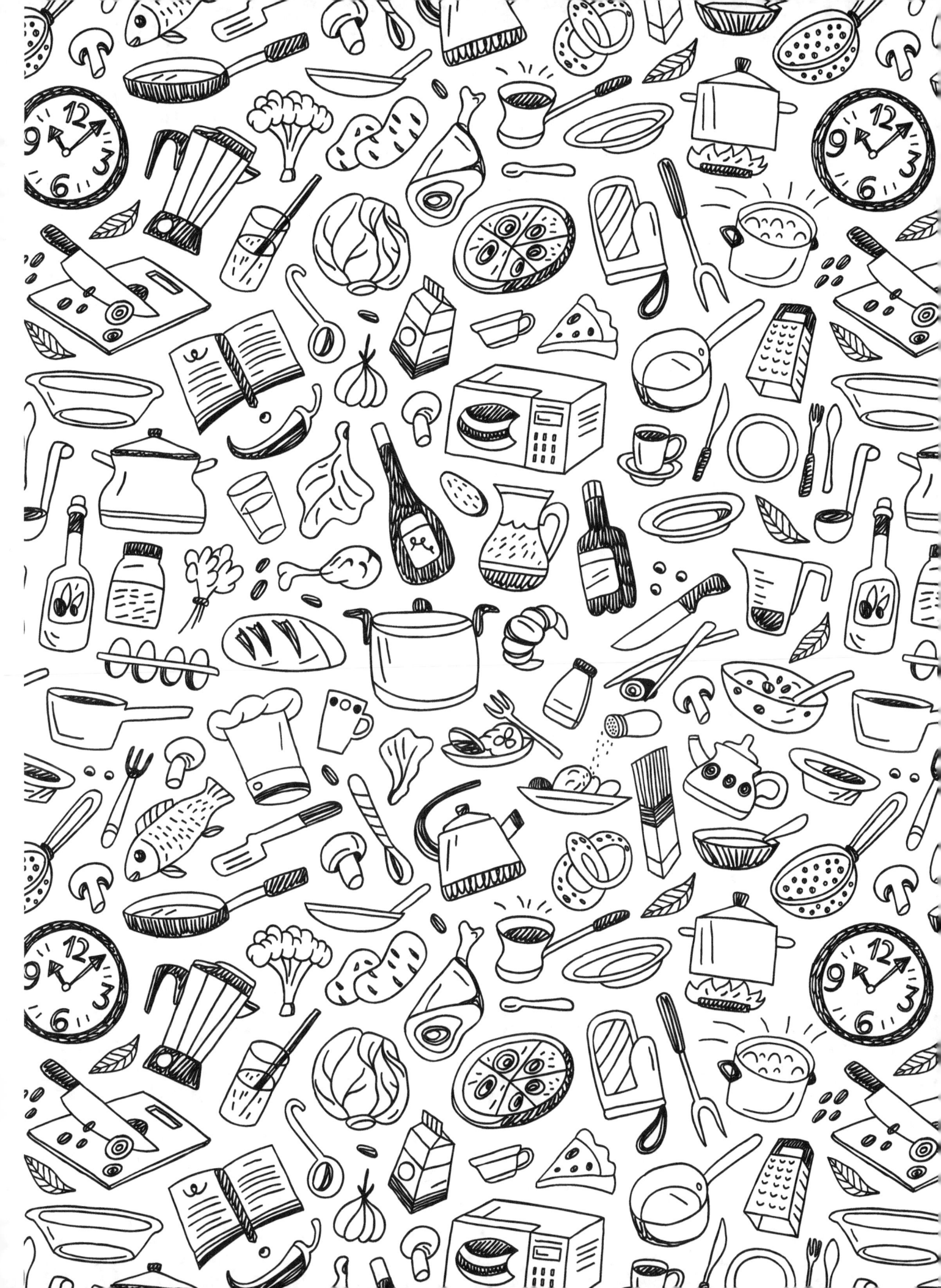

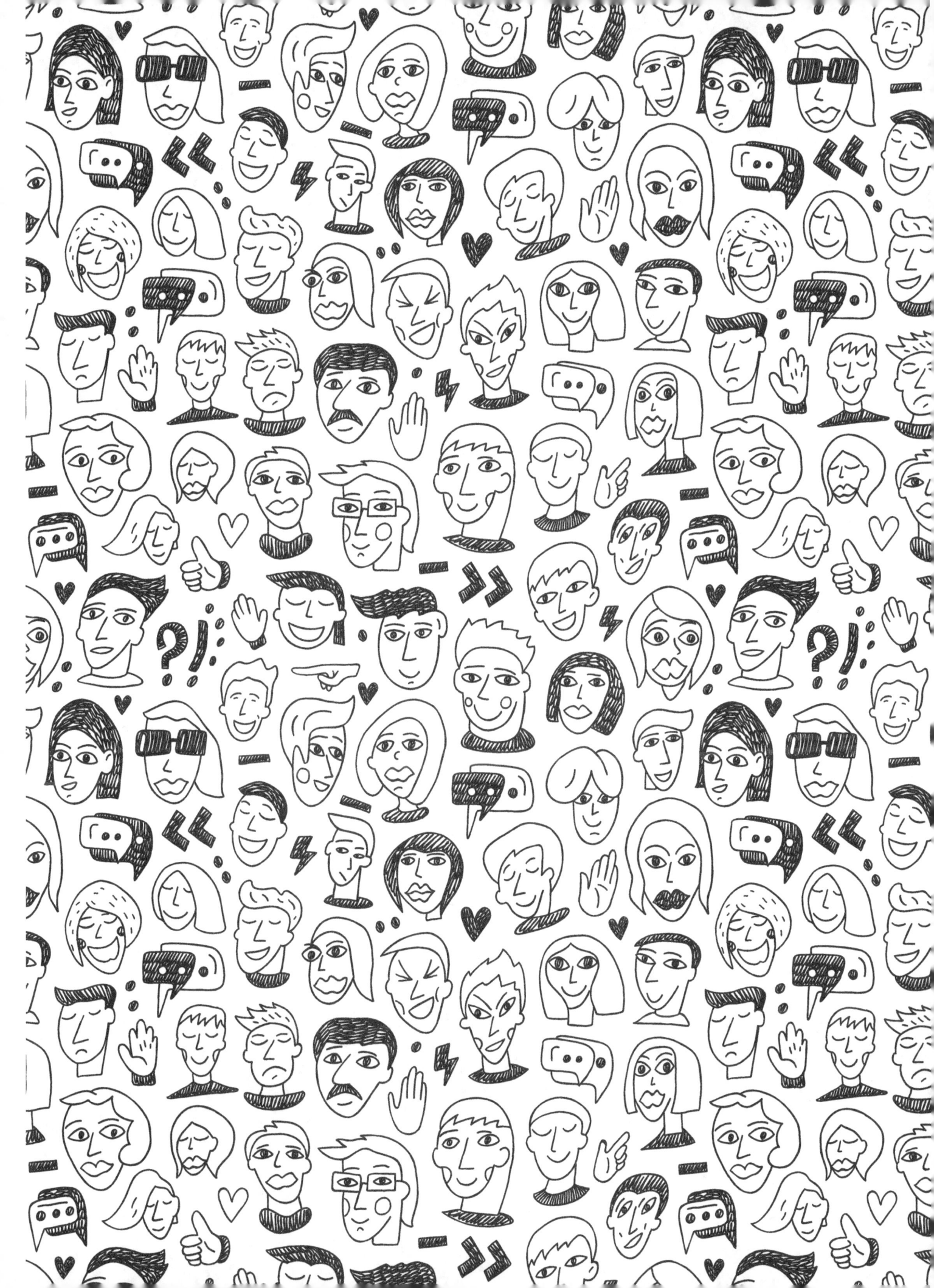

SUPERMARKET

food *drink*

fruit

SUPERMARKET

vegetables

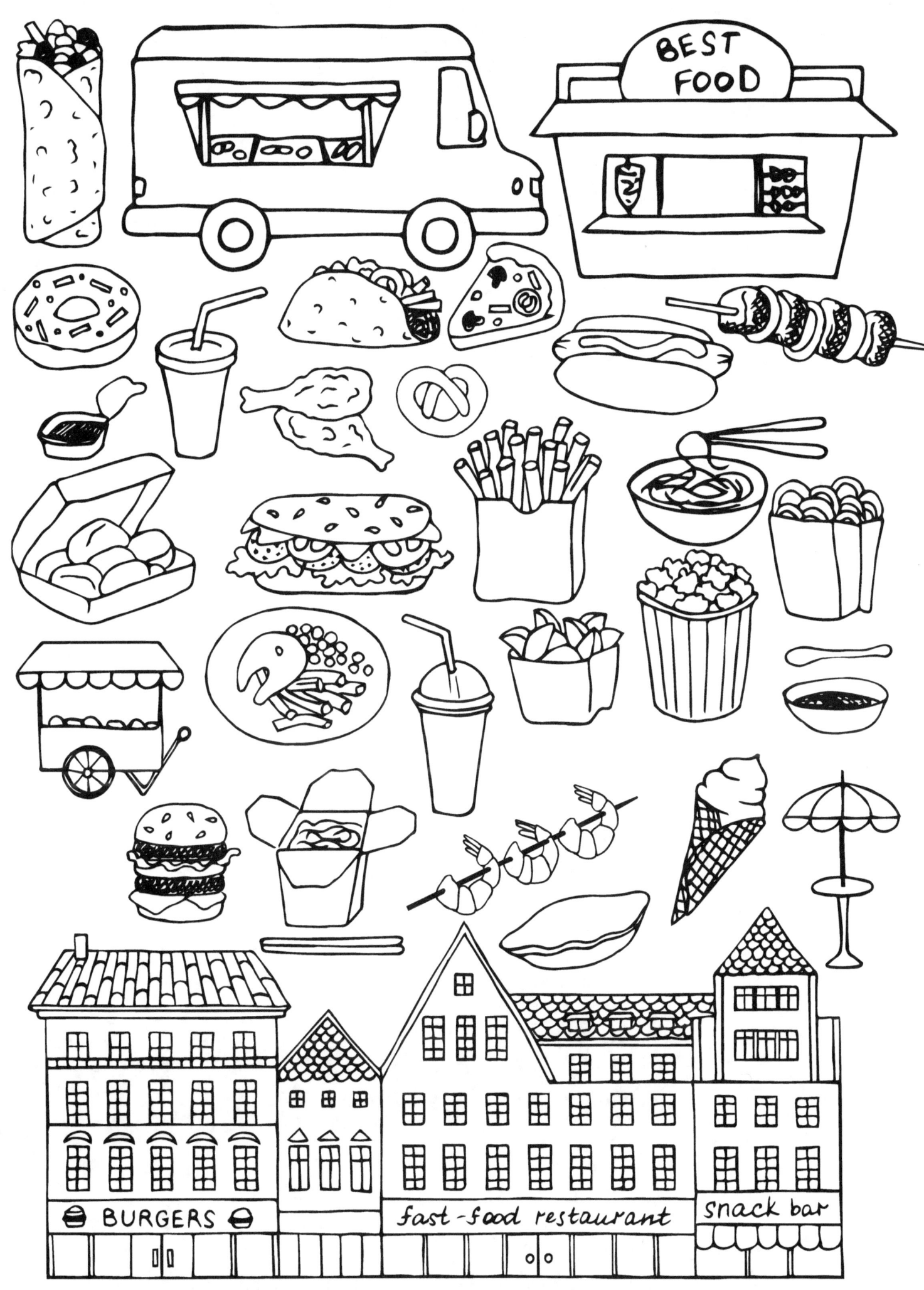

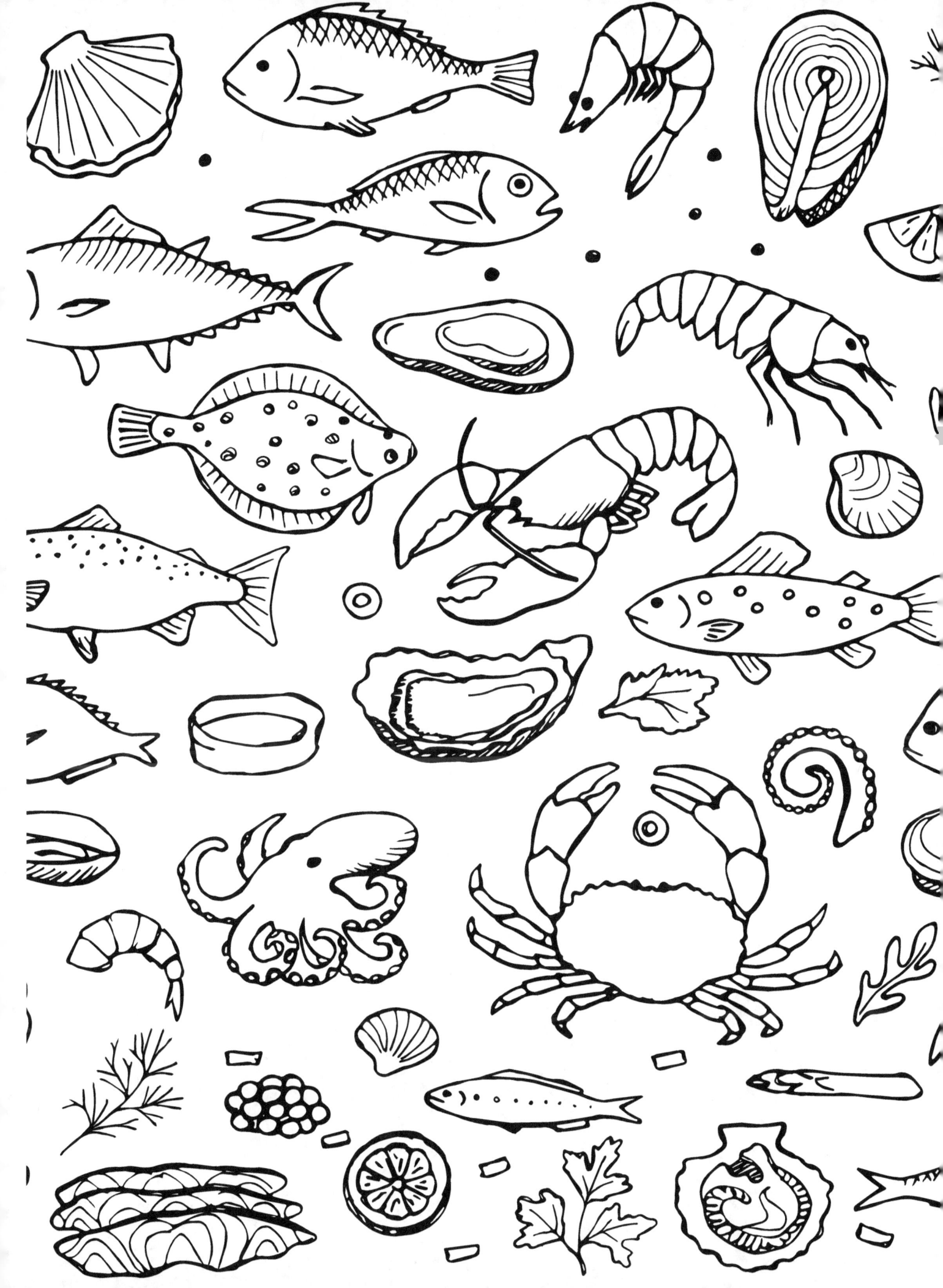

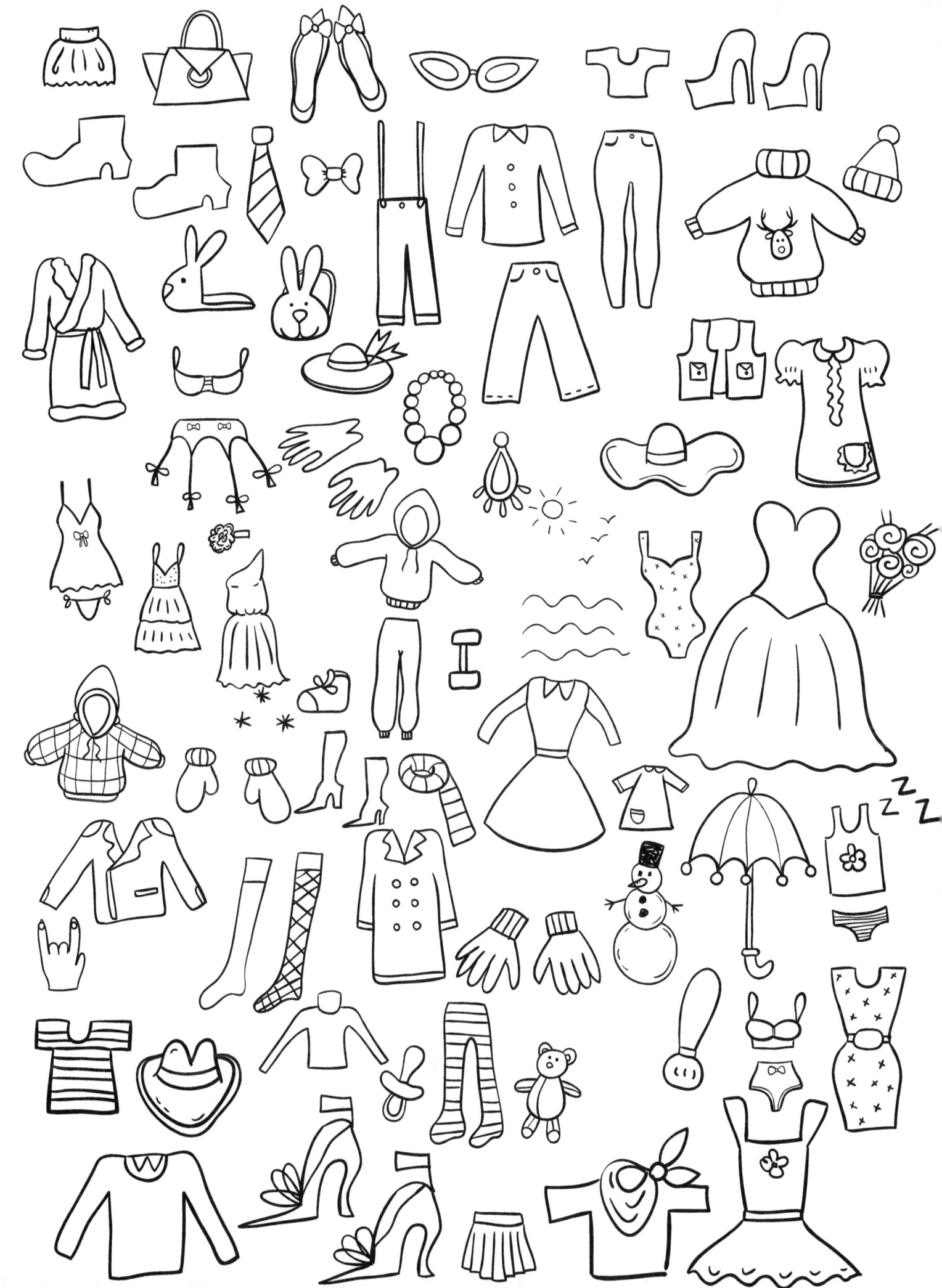

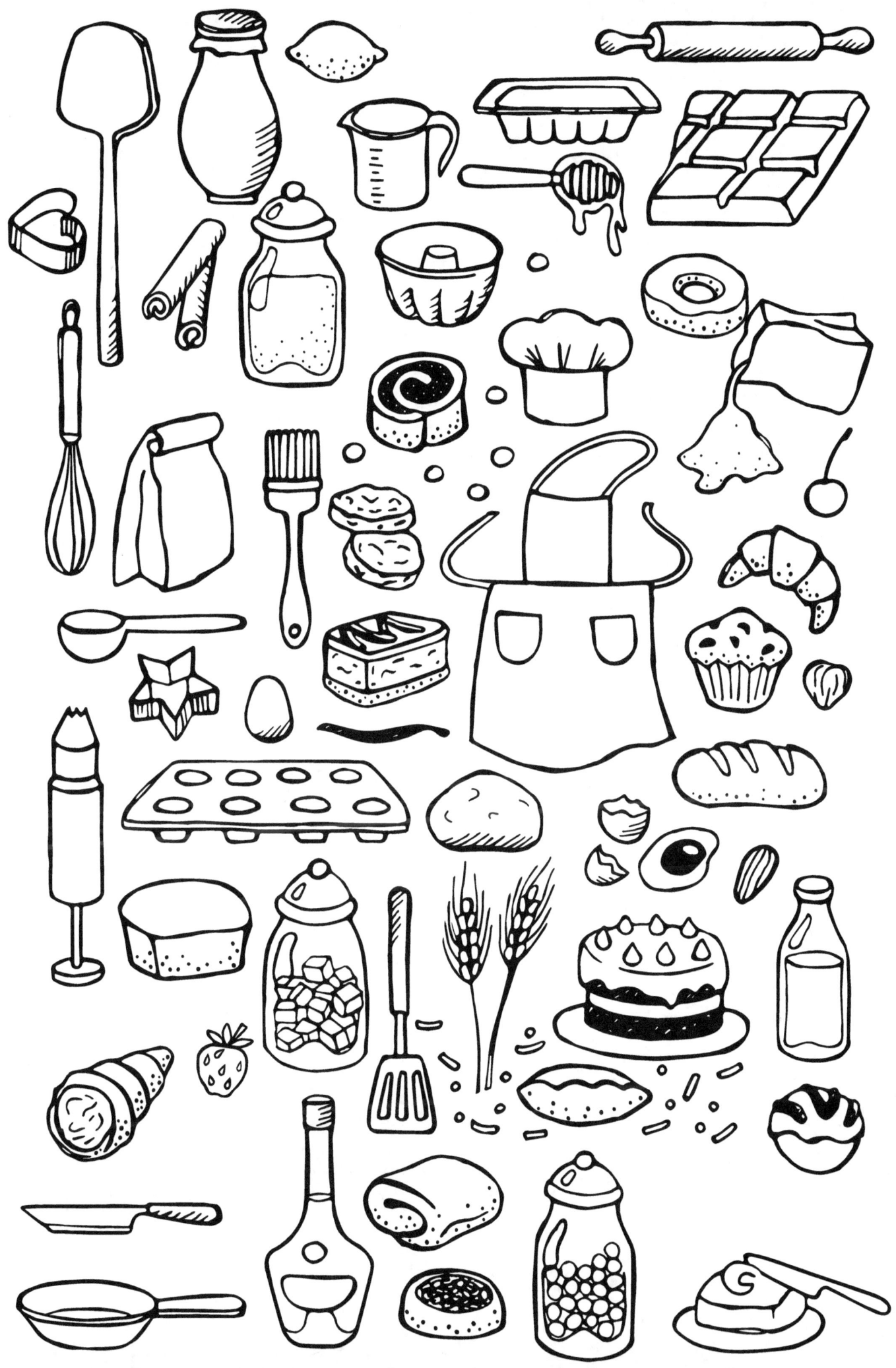

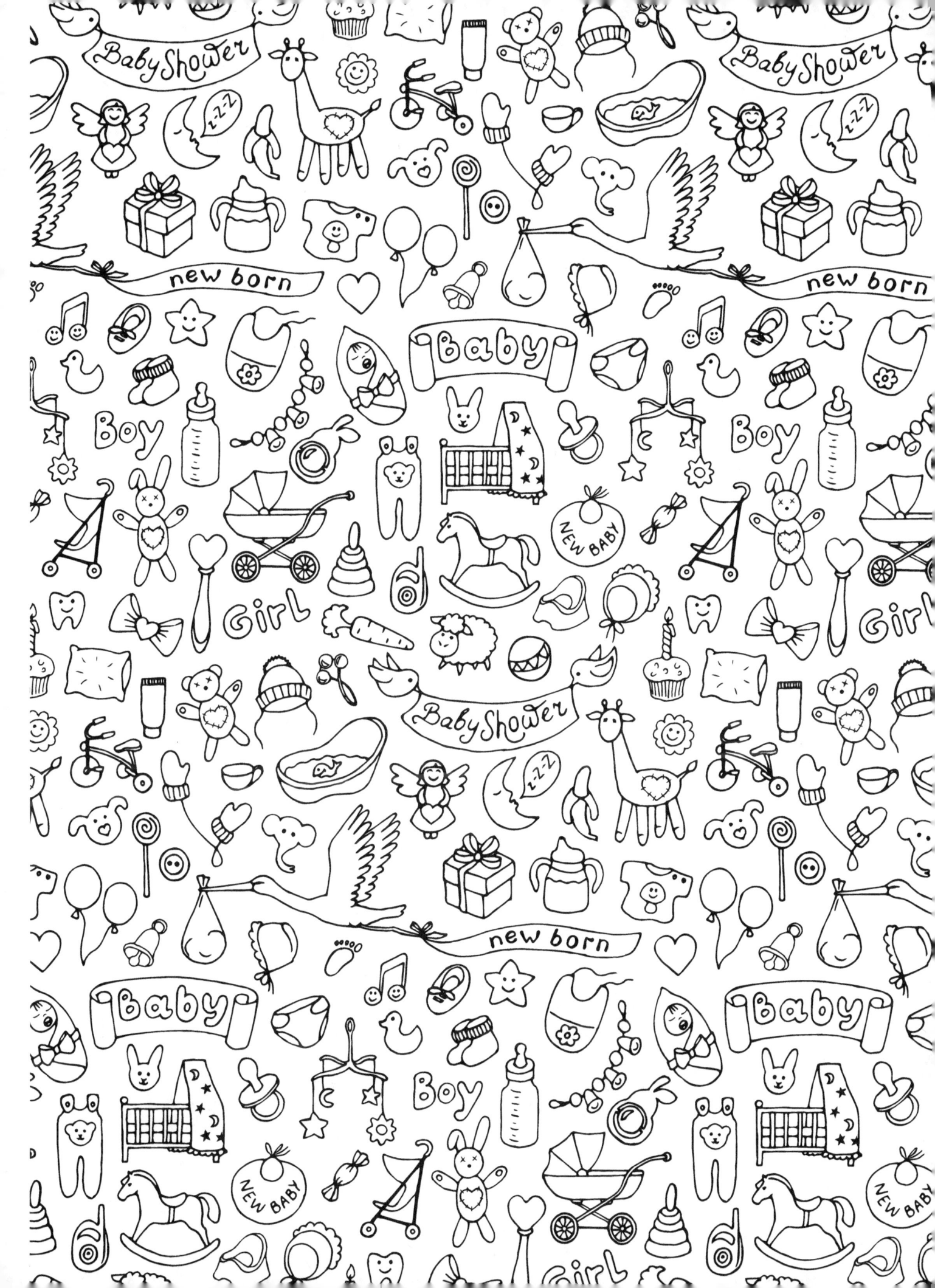

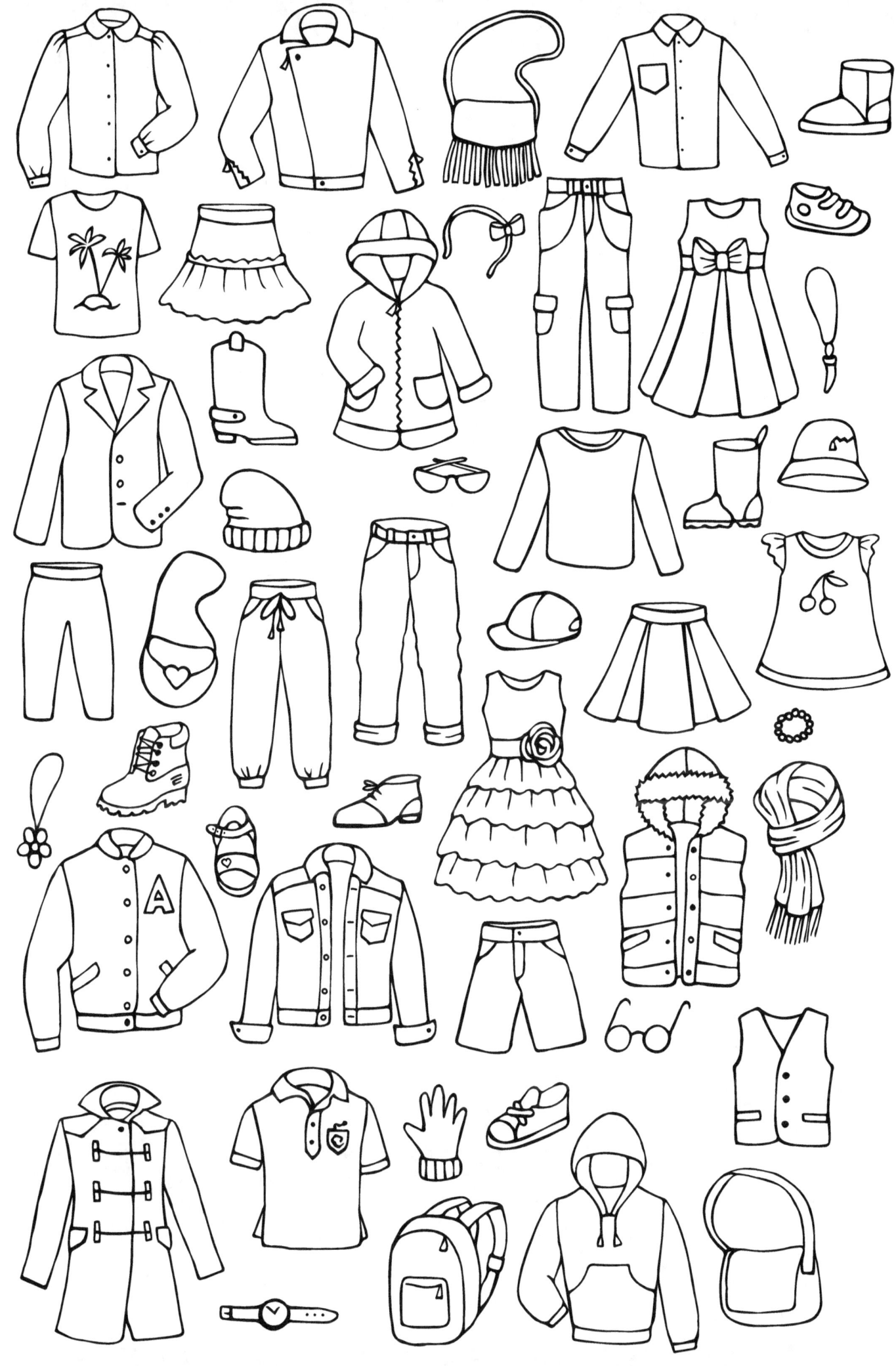

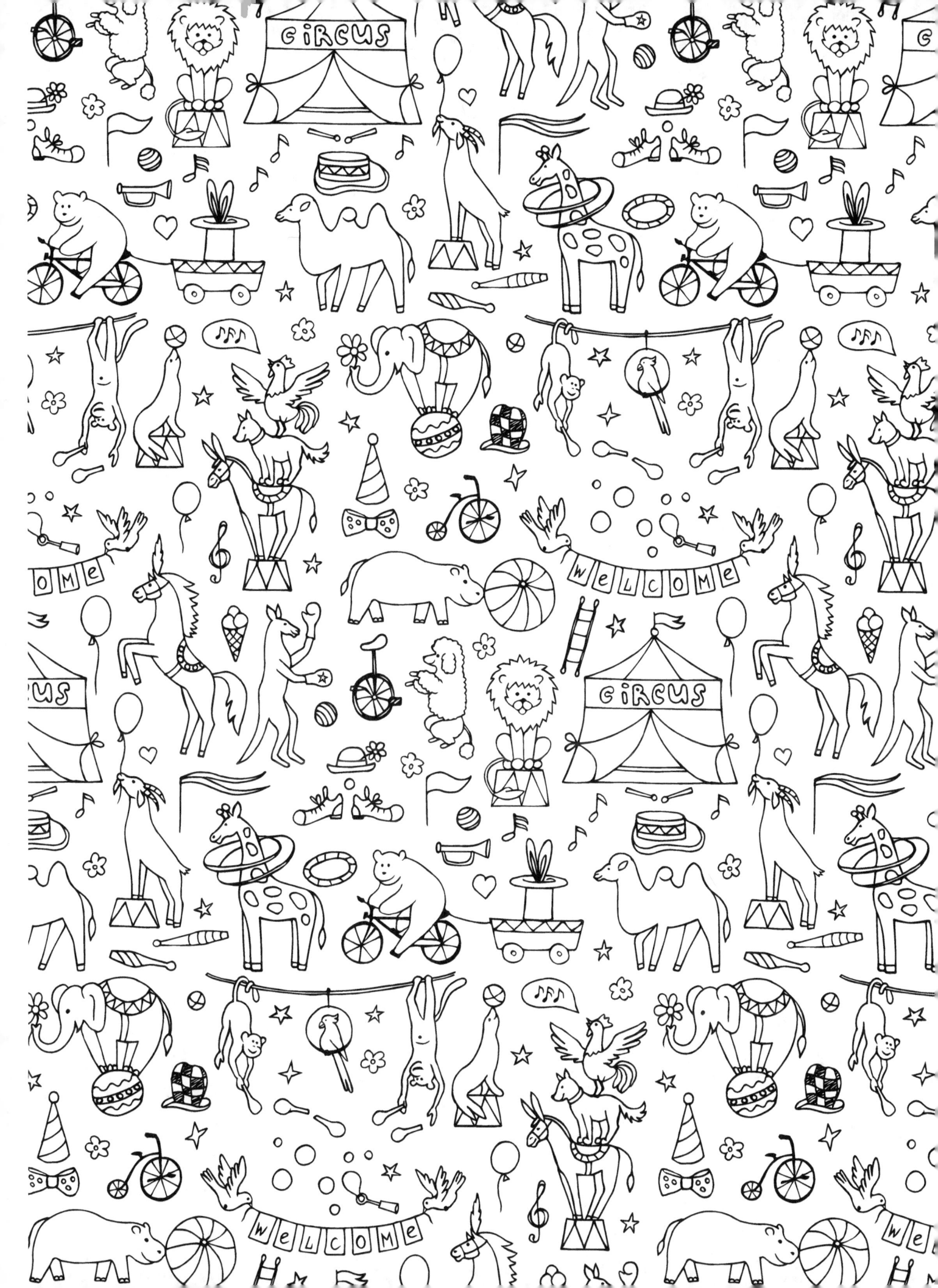

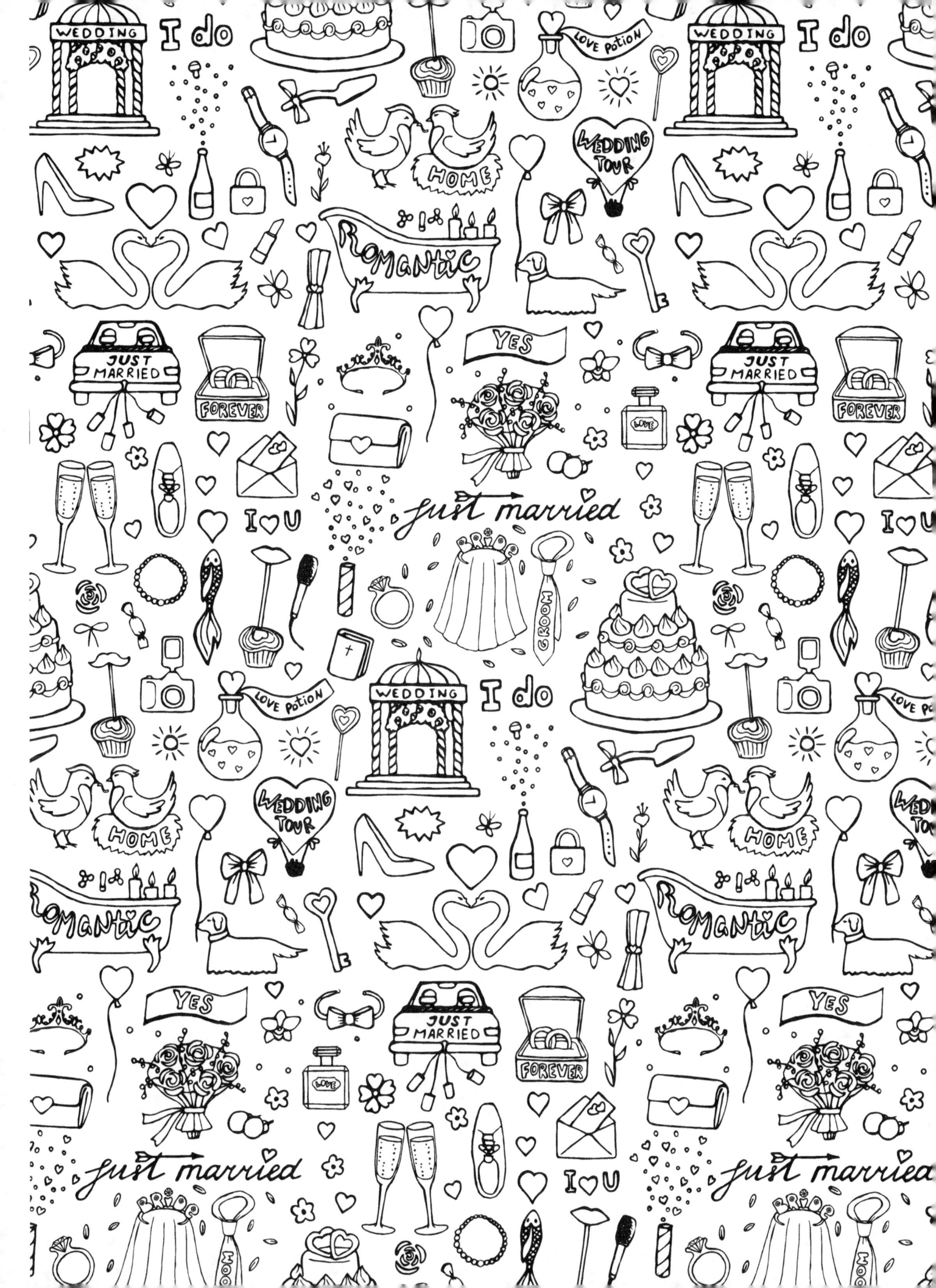

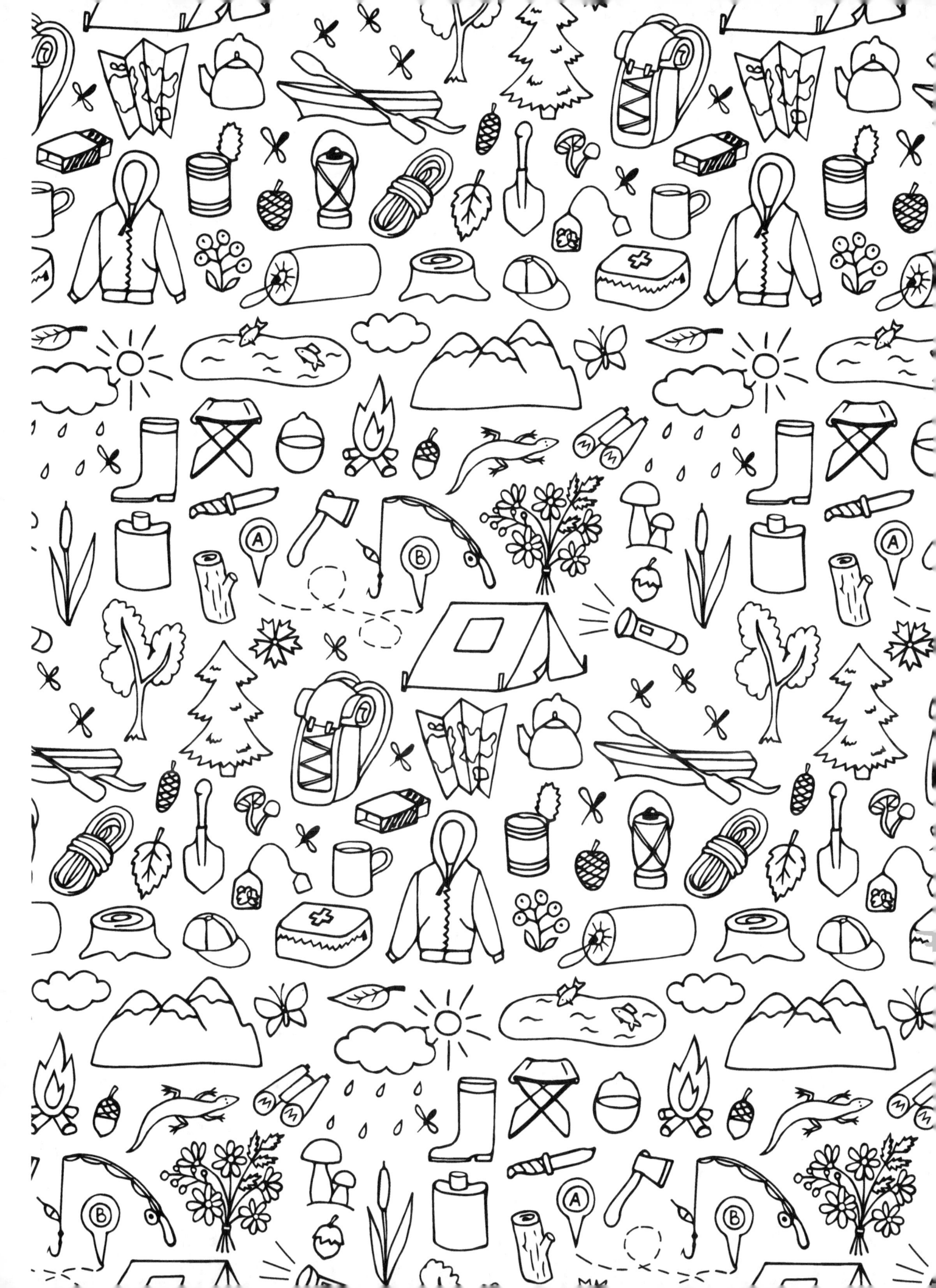

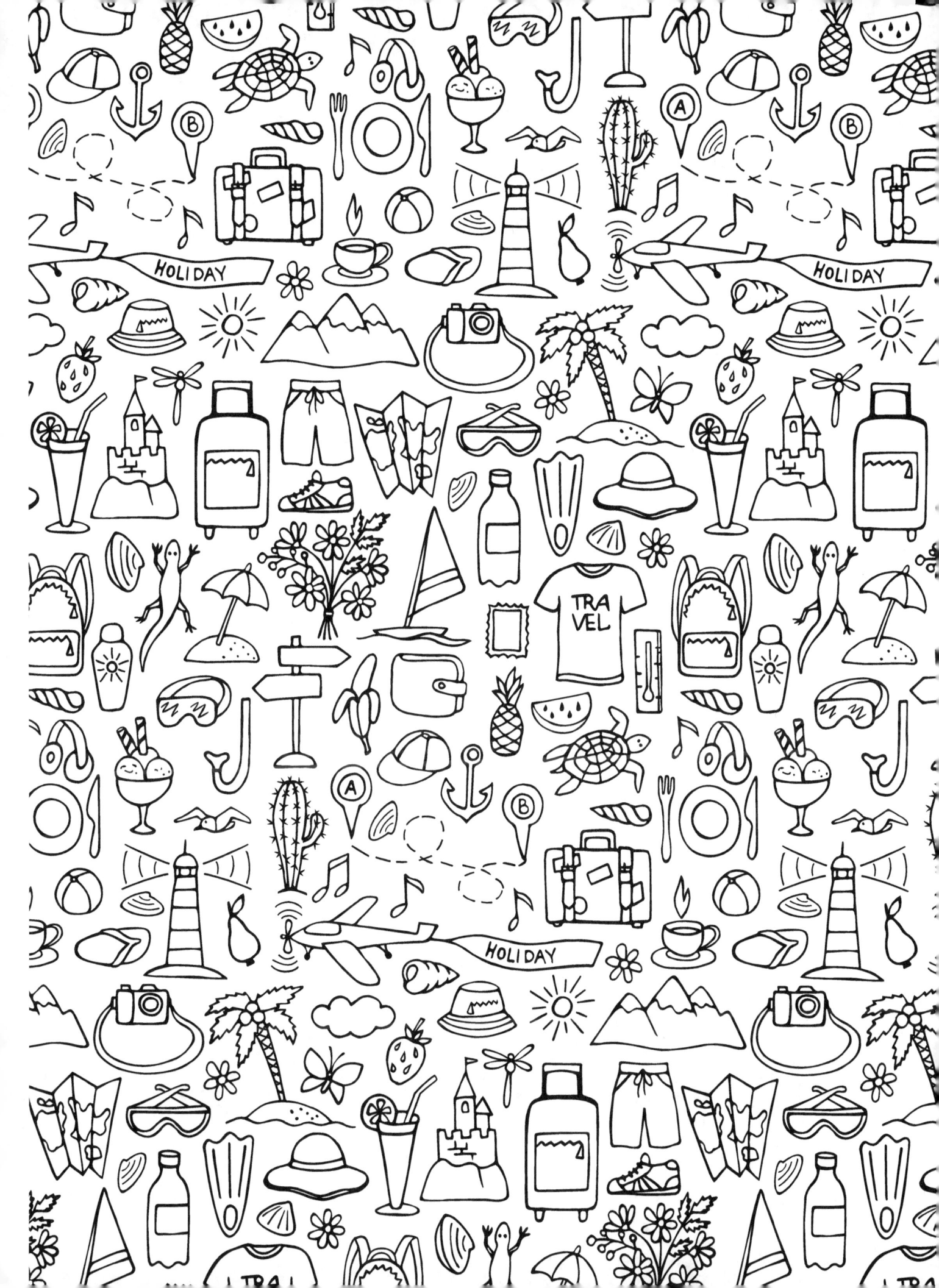

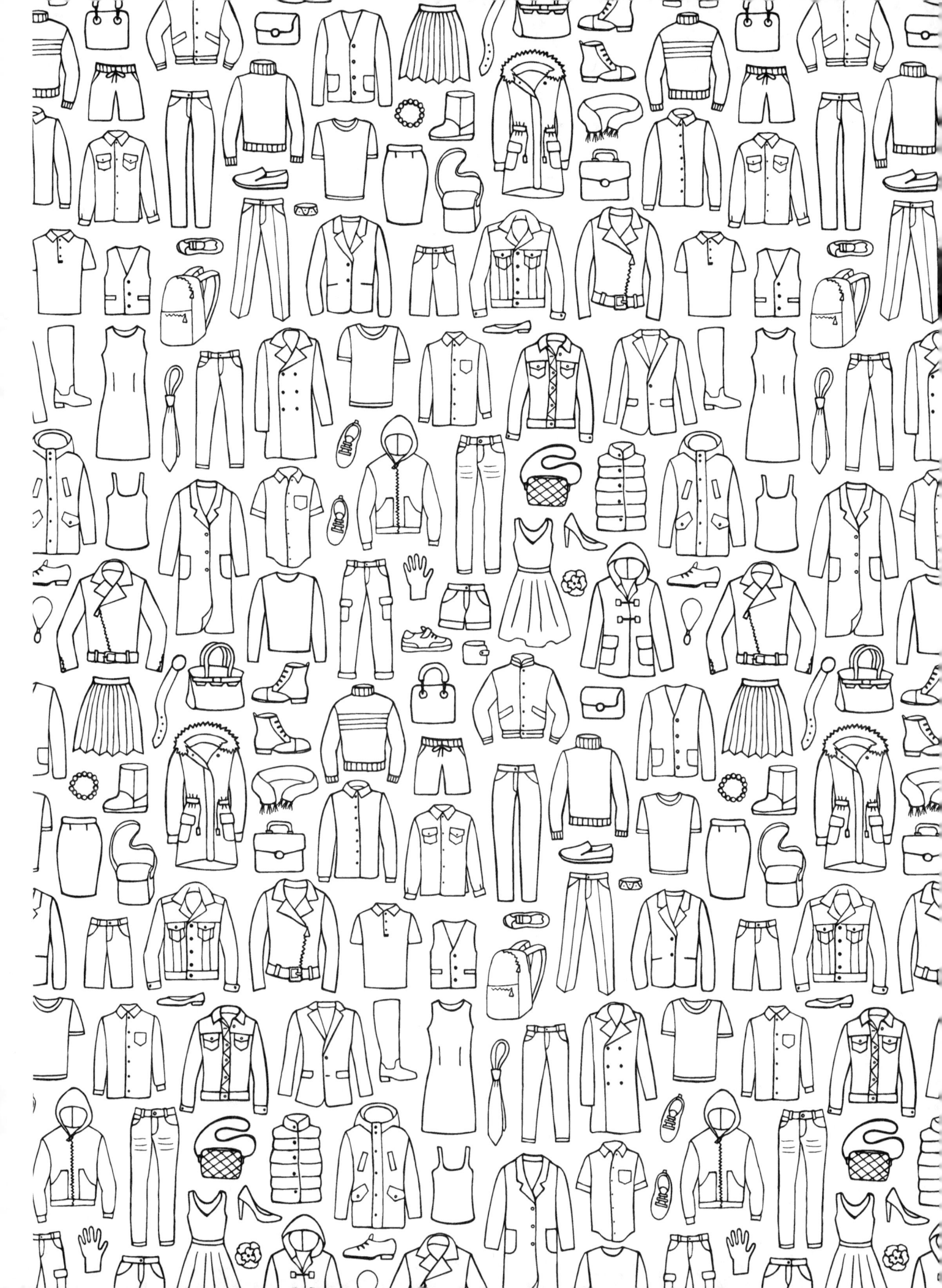

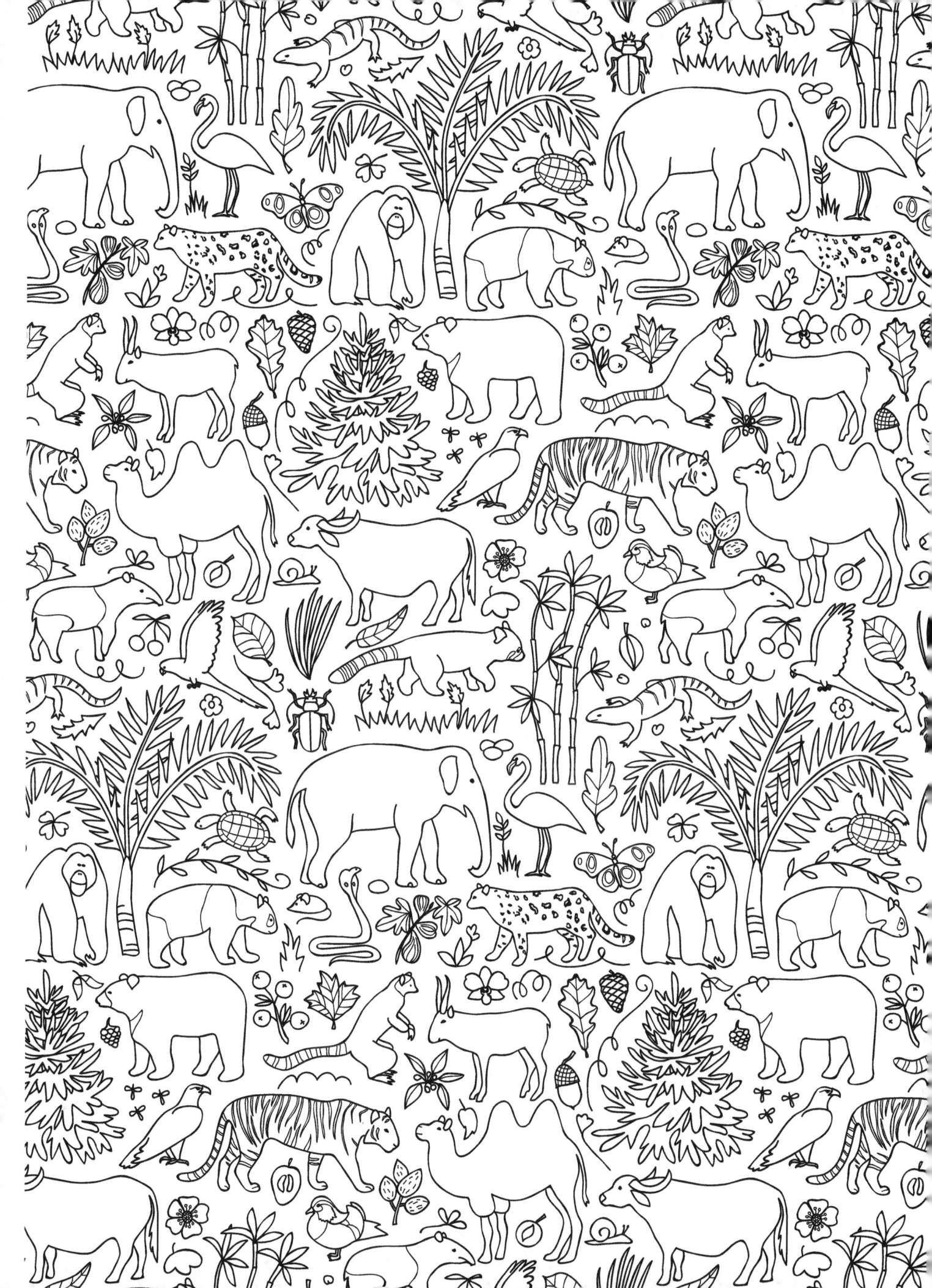

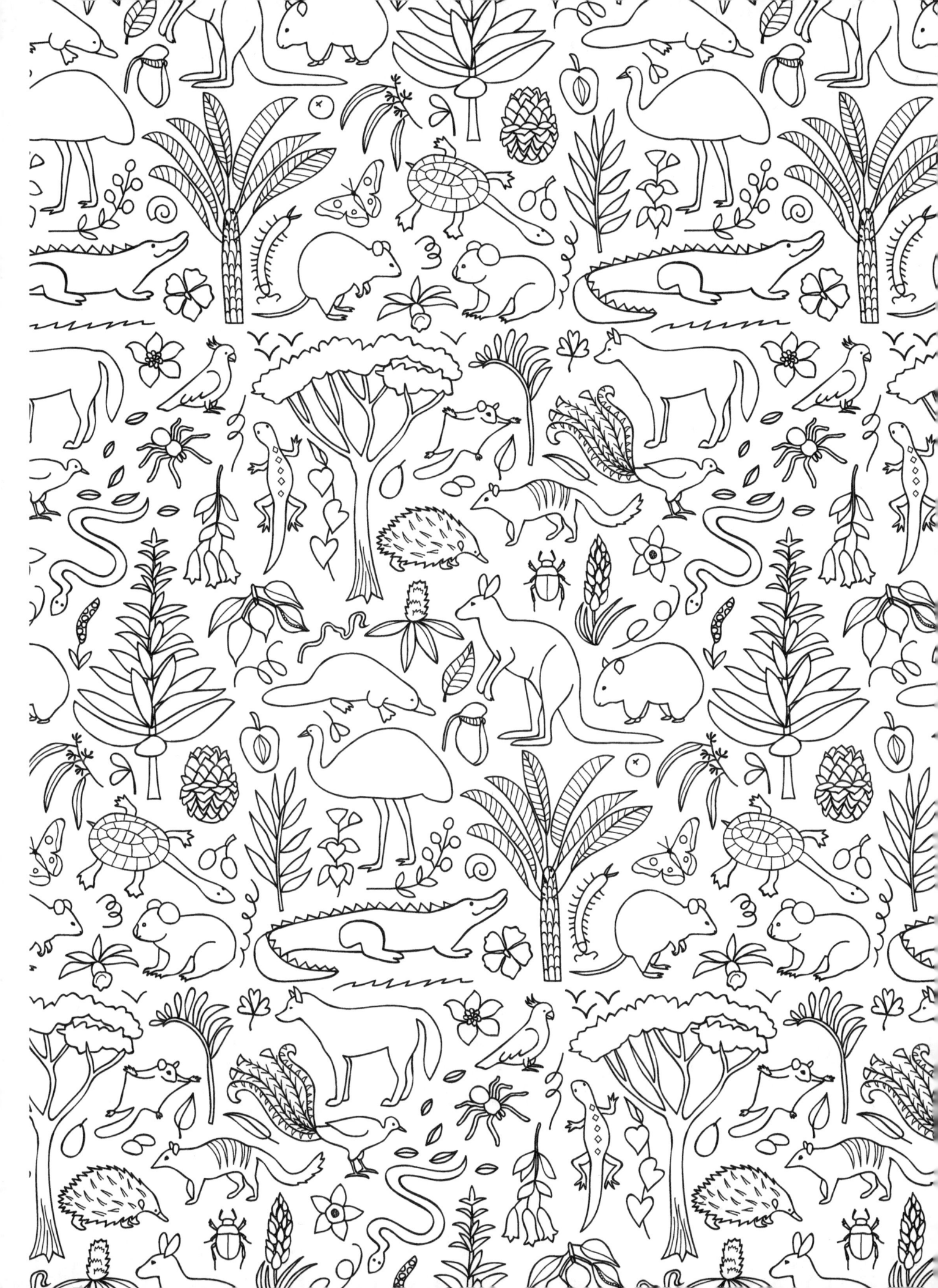

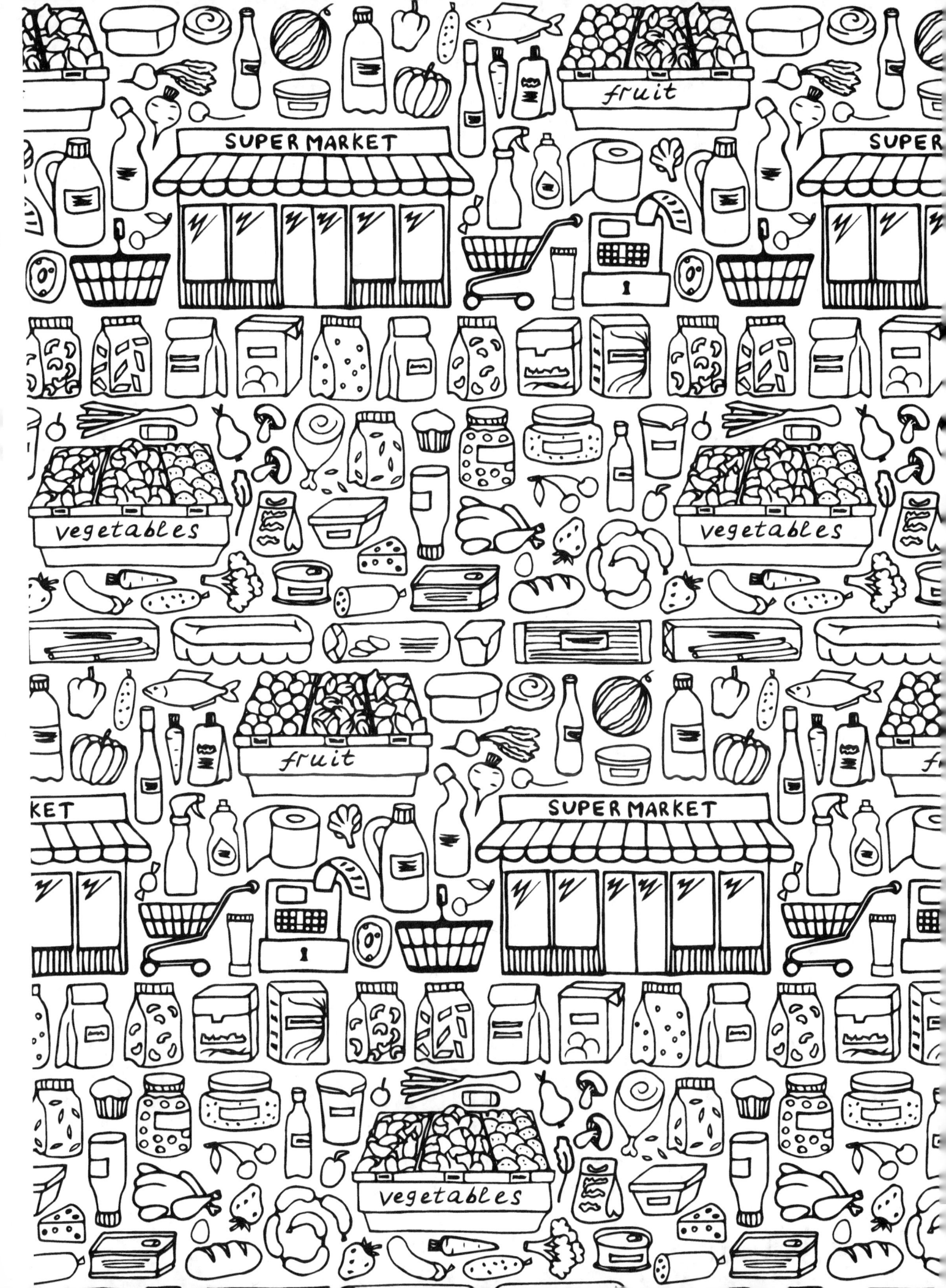

www.ingramcontent.com/pod-product-compliance
Lightning Source LLC
Chambersburg PA
CBHW062339220526
45469CB00008B/2771